PORTRAIT OF
THE ENGLISH RIVIERA

ADRIAN OAKES

HALSGROVE

First published in Great Britain in 2011

British Library Cataloguing-in-Publication Data
A CIP record for this title is available from the British Library

ISBN 978 0 85704 094 7

HALSGROVE
Halsgrove House,
Ryelands Business Park,
Bagley Road, Wellington, Somerset TA21 9PZ
Tel: 01823 653777   Fax: 01823 216796
email: sales@halsgrove.com

Part of the Halsgrove group of companies.
Information on all Halsgrove titles is available at: www.halsgrove.com

Printed in China by Everbest Printing Co Ltd

CONTENTS

MAP OF TORBAY

St Marychurch

● TORQUAY

Babbacombe

Cockington

Preston

● PAIGNTON

The Harbour

Goodrington

DEVON

● Exeter

CORNWALL

Plymouth

TORBAY

Broadsands

Berry Head

● BRIXHAM

INTRODUCTION

STRETCHING ALONG 22 miles of prime Devon coastline The English Riviera has been a popular area with visitors from early Victorian times. It has wonderful beaches, rocky coves, historical buildings, visitor attractions, picturesque harbours and best of all, a mild climate.

The Torquay area first gained a reputation as a destination for relaxation and convalescence during the Napoleonic Wars in the late eighteenth century, but it was the Victorians that coined the phrase 'The English Riviera', likening the area to its French equivalent; sub tropical plants and the famous Torbay palm adding to the bay's Mediterranean feel.

The English Riviera resort towns of Torquay, Paignton and Brixham lie, like a bejewelled necklace, around one of the most beautiful bays in England, each of these communities possessing their own characteristics and charms.

Torquay. The quintessential English resort and often referred to as 'The Queen of the English Riviera', Torquay was the birth place and home of Agatha Christie and is steeped in history as witnessed by evidence of prehistoric man in the spectacular caves of Kents Cavern. The town is famed for its position amongst seven green hills from which Victorian villas and terraces look across the bay. Inland from Torquay is the historical and charming village of Cockington.

Paignton. Famous for its open, sandy, paddle-friendly beaches and its historic and colourful pier, Paignton has remained a popular seaside resort with its lively seafront, Goodrington Sands with its visitor attractions, arcades and Quay West Waterpark.

Brixham. This historical and bustling fishing port sits at the southern tip of Torbay. From the colourful cottages surrounding the harbour to the elegant Marina, Brixham has enchanted visitors for generations.

In September 2007 the English Riviera received international recognition for its rich geological, historical and cultural heritage when it was endorsed by UNESCO, as a European and Global Geopark. Only 67 of these exist in the world.

The geology of the English Riviera has created the beautiful coastline of today, linking the rich diversity of landscape with its wildlife, people and culture.

The shape of the Bay provided the naval fleet safety during times of crisis and thus was a catalyst for the building of the Napoleonic Forts at Berry Head, while its sheltered natural harbours led to the growth of what, at one point, became the UK's largest fishing port. The beauty of the area influenced the early development of a tourism industry that remains buoyant today.

I have visited the English Riviera at all times of the day, throughout the seasons, to capture the images for this book. During that time I discovered a great many interesting places and facts about the English Riviera which I hope the reader will enjoy too.

Adrian Oakes 2011
www.adrianoakes.com

Torquay harbour taken from the Terrace and looking over the shops below. Preston beach, Paignton, Goodrington and Broadsands can all be clearly identified in the distance.

TORQUAY

Torquay Pavilion and the fountain in the attractive gardens opposite. The Pavilion opened in 1912 as a 'Palace of Pleasure' to attract visitors to Torquay. It was used for music and plays, and as a meeting place. It is one of the best remaining examples of Victorian seaside architecture and was designed by Major Henry Augustus Garrett. It was not built on the pier, as many pavilions were, but adjoining it. It was originally called 'The Cucumber House' when it was being built in 1889 and became known as 'The White Palace' due to its white exterior tiles which were made by Royal Doulton. The original cost of building the pavilion was £16942 4s 4d. It currently houses a unique collection of speciality shops and galleries.

Evening light cast on the striking white tiles and copper roofing of Torquay Pavilion.

A magnificent view of Torquay harbour and the hill behind seen from a height of 400 feet. This image, along with some others in this book, was taken from the immensely popular Torquay 'Hi-Flyer' helium balloon which ascends from the Torre Abbey Gardens.

Warm evening light and reflections at Torquay inner harbour. Low tide is a thing of the past in the inner harbour. The waterfront underwent a £21 million redevelopment and the original harbour bed is no longer uncovered at each tide. The water in the inner harbour is kept at mid-tide with the use of a cill gate.

Sparkling lights illuminate the Princess Pier, Torquay on a mild autumn evening. The lights produce little sun stars in the photograph due to the small aperture used when the image was taken.

Opposite: Torquay seafront showing the Princess Pier and the old original railings that run the length of the promenade.

THE BABBACOMBE MODEL VILLAGE

The outdoor model village was opened in 1963 by Tom Dobbins. Mr Dobbins had previously opened another model village at Southport in 1957. The site covers 4 acres and includes over 400 models along with over 1000ft (300m) of model train track.

Top right: The same houses as appear in the image on the opposite page (below) but taken at Christmas with the customary coating of snow that appears every year, transforming the model village into a Winter Wonderland enjoyed by all ages.

Bottom right: Another snow scene. The attention to detail is amazing and the Model Village is well worth a look at any time of year.

A fine example of traditional architecture, elegant townhouses in Torquay.

Opposite: Interesting shadows cast by the low afternoon sun of the palm trees in Torre Abbey Gardens taken from above. The Torquay palms are very much a symbol of the area. Originally imported from New Zealand in the 1820s by plant collectors they can be found all around the English Riviera.

Torre Abbey seen from the air. Torre Abbey dates back to 1196 and has survived and played a role in some epic moments in history. The Catholic Cary family bought the abbey in 1662 after a succession of owners and lived there for 268 years. It is the largest surviving medieval monastery in Devon and Cornwall. It is divided into 122 rooms over 20 different levels which means negotiating 265 steps.

The abbey also boasts another of the English Riviera's most famous buildings, the Spanish Barn – a medieval tithe barn originally built to store taxes paid to the abbey in the form of grain, hay and other produce. The barn's place in history was firmly established at the time of the Spanish Armada in 1588 when 400 Spanish prisoners from a captured galleon were held here. Taking the photograph from above has enabled me to capture both buildings in their full glory.

A colourful winter sunset over Torquay harbour.

Torbay looking from above Torquay harbour towards Brixham and Berry Head. A cargo ship waits in the bay to unload its goods. Berry Head lighthouse sits on the headland just above it with Brixham just to the right.

Looking over Torquay Pavilion towards Goodrington. Broadsands, and the long row of beach huts, can be seen in the centre of the picture.

Opposite: The beautiful Victorian 'Friends Fountain' in the Gardens near Torquay Pavilion, bathed in evening light.

Corbyn Head beach in summer. The neat little beach huts sit on stilts to keep them out of harm's way at high tide.

A Summer's morning looking from Meadfoot beach.

Left: The bronze bust of Agatha Christie in Cary Gardens near the Pavilion. Agatha Mary Clarissa Miller was born in Torquay on 15 September 1890 and lived most of her life in the area. She is the best selling author of all time having sold over 2 billion books. Agatha Christie wrote 80 novels and short story collections.

Looking across Peaked Tor cove from Torquay Marina, with the Milestones rocks in the foreground.

HARBOUR BRIDGE

Contrasting views of Torquay's futuristic Harbour footbridge taken in daylight and at night.

A bird's-eye view taken from the Torquay 'Hi-Flyer'. I like this picture because of the elements included in it; the gardens on the cliff tops, the new Rock Walk illuminated steps, the Princess Theatre, the inner harbour and the Pavilion.

Christmas at Torquay harbour with the illuminated Harbour Bridge in the background.

Right: Early morning at Meadfoot rocks as a small fishing vessel returns to port.

30

COCKINGTON VILLAGE

Cockington Village on a warm Spring morning. I took this opportunity to take a panoramic photograph of the village centre after the horses and carriages had taken visitors for trips round the village. I then took some photographs of the carriages on their return, as shown overleaf.

Top: Cockington Village in full Spring bloom with the Old School House sitting to the right of the picture.

Left: Cockington appears in the Domesday Book. Here the popular horse-drawn carriages wait for tourists in the heart of the village which sits only a mile from Torquay seafront. The quaint thatched buildings (even the public toilets are thatched) make Cockington one of the most photographed places in the country.

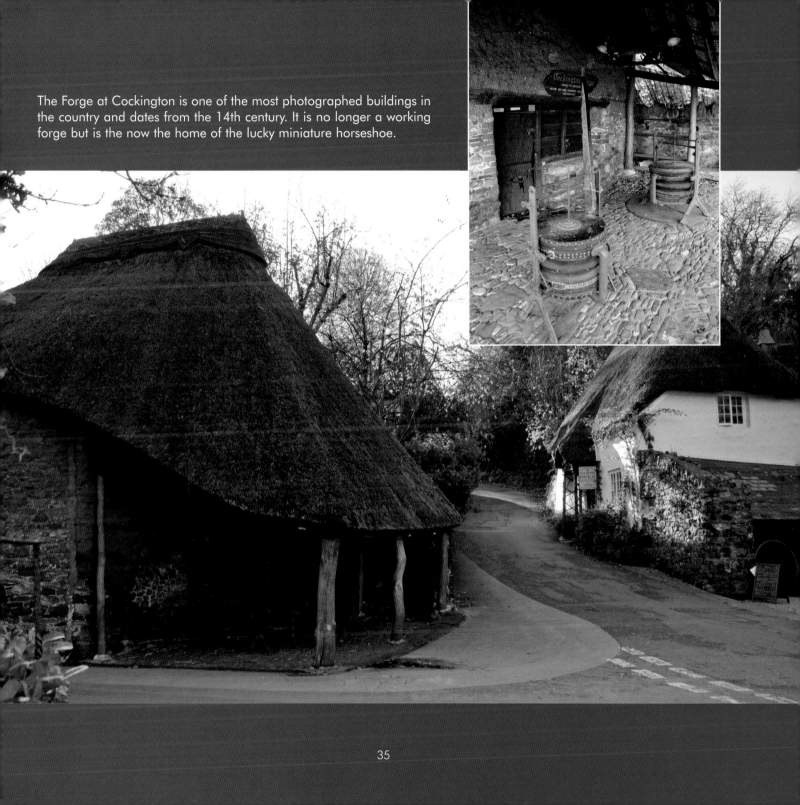

The Forge at Cockington is one of the most photographed buildings in the country and dates from the 14th century. It is no longer a working forge but is the now the home of the lucky miniature horseshoe.

Torquay inner harbour. This image caught my eye because of the myriad of different reflections.

Walkway at Torquay Marina.

Right: Striking skies over luxury hilltop apartments above Torquay marina.

Torquay inner harbour tranquillity. Still water created by the cill gate and lack of wind adds pleasant reflections to the image. The cill gate sits below the striking footbridge and drops as the bridge rises to allow boats to leave the inner harbour.

Just one of the impressive views I enjoyed from 400 feet above Torquay in the 'Hi-Flyer'. Haytor on Dartmoor sits on the horizon, clearly visible from many miles away.

'Millionaires Row' in Torquay harbour. The helium filled 'Hi-Flyer' nestles in the background, in between flights.

An atmospheric corner of Torbay. These concrete steps, just along from Oddicombe beach, must see very little sun.

Opposite: Oddicombe beach which is the home of the Babbacombe Cliff Railway. A 5000 ton rock fall from February 2010 spreads out over the far end of the beach below.

The Harbour Master's HQ looking over Torquay harbour.

Left: Old and New. Old cast iron uprights hold modern railings at the end of Princess Pier, Torquay. They show many, many layers of weathered paint.

This striking wooden walkway caught my eye during a stroll along the coast to Babbacombe village which sits in the background.

Previous pages: View towards Paignton from the Rock Walk.

Opposite: The wonderful neon-like glow from the illuminated steps and icons.

Left: The steps connect Rock Walk with the Royal Terrace Gardens. The walk was originally opened in the 1800s and was a winding set of steps to the terrace at the top of the cliff. Due to cliff instability the walk was closed and huge amounts of vegetation were removed in 2008. The extensive works to stabilise the cliff led to the gardens and impressive illuminated steps being constructed. They were opened in Autumn 2010.

Below: View of the harbour from the Rock Walk steps. The long exposure had created an eerie blue glow around the illuminated insets on each step.

Part of the extensive refurbishment of Torquay harbour in 2003 included the construction of this very striking state-of-the-art footbridge which allows people to walk all the way round the harbour. The clever part is that the bridge includes an underwater cill gate which, when the bridge is lifted, moves downwards to allow vessels safe passage. The water in the harbour is permanently kept at mid-tide.

Left: Princess Pier on the edge of Torquay harbour. Designed initially in 1890 as a simple concrete groyne, the lattice steelwork and timber decking were added to the structure in 1894, together with the wooden landing stage on the seaward side of the pierhead in 1906. Agatha Christie roller-skated on the pier as a young girl.

Amazing photos can often be found in the most unlikely of places. Whilst walking along the promenade from Corbyn beach, I came across a huge 'puddle'. Passers by watched in bewilderment as I was lying on my stomach with my elbows in the puddle taking pictures. I was after this reflection.

Boats sit motionless on a bright and sunny Spring day at Torquay inner harbour.

Left: Wonderful panoramic image of summer skies looking from Corbyn Head.

Just a short stroll from Babbacombe reveals the historic village of St Marychurch. The pretty Victorian style pedestrian precinct offers a wide choice of shops and boutiques. This is the site of two landmark churches that make up Torquay's skyline. This picture was taken from the top of the precinct at Christmas.

Opposite, top: Night time illuminations at Torquay harbour.

Opposite, bottom: This long-exposure shot was taken just before Christmas from Torquay Marina looking towards the Pavilion with the illuminated Rock Walk in the distance.

Looking out to Thatcher Rock just after sunrise. Filters were used in this image to slow the shutter speed creating the misty effect around the rocks. It was, in fact, a very rough sea with a difficult climb down to the rocks.

View from above Torquay of the Harbour bridge, Princess Theatre and the 'Hi-Flyer'.

KENTS CAVERN

Kents Cavern is a spectacular natural cave in Torquay and undoubtedly one of the most special caves in the country. The incredible geology and rich archaeological heritage of the cave has been astounding scientists and visitors alike for centuries.

Records show the mysteries of the caves have been enticing explorers to venture into their depths since 1571. However, archaeological evidence and research reveals that people and animals had been visiting the caves for hundreds of thousands of years in prehistory.

Kents Cavern is a gateway visitor centre for UNESCO's English Riviera Global Geopark. The Geopark reveals a geological story that goes back 400 million years and one which has shaped the landscape and cultural heritage of the area. Kents Cavern is a protected national site because it is by far the most important prehistoric cave dwelling in Britain and is known throughout the world for its archaeological record of prehistoric human life.

View of the now closed Palm Court Hotel and the public walk bridge near Torre Abbey gardens. The terrace was built as Abbey Crescent between 1856 and 1858 on Cary Estate land and later became the hotel.

Overleaf: Crystal clear water and reflections of the yachts at Torquay Marina in July.

A fishing trawler returns to port just after sunrise. Torquay's Thatcher Rock sits on the horizon.

The Torbay 'Hi-Flyer' rises above Torre Abbey Gardens. The balloon, based near the gardens, is a passenger carrying helium balloon tethered to the ground by a cable and winch. The balloon is 72 feet in diameter and 120 feet high and reaches a maximum flying height of 400 feet for spectacular uninterrupted views of Torbay and the surrounding countryside, including Dartmoor.

Right: A classic view looking along the original wrought iron seating on Princess Pier. Ornate lamps sit at intervals along the pier's length.

A spectacular panoramic view of Torquay marina from 400 feet. From here you can see the entirety of the Princess Pier and the Harbour walls. The Milestone rocks and Peak Tor Cove lie in the distance.

The Living Coasts attraction can be seen just at the end of the main harbour wall in the very centre of the photograph.

A long exposure creates wonderful colourful reflections in the sea below the Grand Hotel.

The Mallock Clock in Torquay Harbour. The clock tower, known as the Mallock Memorial, was built in 1902 and is named after Richard Mallock, who died in 1900. The Mallocks lived in Cockington and helped to develop Torquay during the nineteenth century. The clock is made of Bath stone and is a well known landmark in Torquay's Strand. The clock has recently undergone a £100 000 restoration during which the bell was rediscovered and will hopefully chime again. The bell had been silent since it was disconnected in 1939 at the start of the war.

Right: Houses nestle gracefully on the hillside amongst the lush trees.

One of the benefits of panoramic images for which I am best known is that a huge field of view is possible. This image shows the northern end of Preston beach and the beach huts.

PAIGNTON

A brief break in the cloud, allows the sun to break through at sunrise at Paignton Pier.

The colourful crazy golf course on Paignton Pier.

Tempting choices on Paignton beach in midsummer.

Right: The Paignton & Dartmouth Steam Railway locomotive leaving Paignton. The picturesque rail line starts its journey close to the colourful beach huts at Goodrington. Here the engine driver waves to holidaymakers on the beach.

A typical seasonal shop on Paignton seafront displaying its wares.

Opposite: Wonderful light and skies looking towards Berry Head from Goodrington Gardens at Roundham Head.

Prizes waiting to be won on Paignton Pier.

TOWER ROAD

COVERDALE TOWER

The Coverdale Tower is adjacent to the Paignton Parish Church and is named after Bishop Miles Coverdale who published an English translation of the Bible in 1536. Coverdale was Bishop of Exeter between 1551 and 1553 and is said to have lived in the tower during this period, although this is regarded as doubtful by modern historians. It sits in the surviving outer fortifications that surrounded the manor house, now demolished. The Church Vicarage and the Parish Hall are sit in the grounds.

Vibrant flower borders and a Torbay palm sit at the entrance to Paignton harbour.

Right: A collection of small colourful boats lie in Paignton harbour at low tide.

The Harbour Light Restaurant and booking offices, early morning, Paignton harbour.

Looking across to Brixham and Berry Head from Goodrington beach on a fine sunny day.

Broadsands is an idyllic beach consisting mainly of sand, ideal for those wishing to distance themselves from amusement arcades. This view was taken looking from the golf course, showing the row of beach huts that run the length of the beach.

The old picture house in Paignton. This was later named the Torbay Cinema. A hotel was demolished on this site to make way for the cinema. It is said to be the oldest purpose-built cinema in Europe and was in continuous use from 1908. It has now sadly closed and is owned by the company the runs the Paignton & Dartmouth Steam Railway. Seat 2 Row 2 of the circle was the favourite seat of crime novelist Agatha Christie, who lived in neighbouring Torquay. The cinemas and theatres in her books are all said to be based on the Torbay Cinema. It was also used as a location for the 1984 Donald Sutherland film *Ordeal by Innocence* and the 1981 film The *French Lieutenant's Woman* (which was filmed largely at Lyme Regis in Dorset).

A stunning floral display over the entrance of the Harbour Light Restaurant that nestles in Paignton harbour.

Left: Distant view of Torbay and the Marina from the Paignton Harbour wall.

Goodrington beach in late summer looking from high up in Goodrington Gardens.

Paignton harbour was established in the thirteenth century and has seen many changes over the centuries. It was a thriving fishing harbour for many years and some of the old traditions of seamanship are kept alive and passed on through generations of Paigntonians. The local council has managed the harbour since 1935.

Today the harbour remains a hive of activity, especially during the summer months, and a vast range of different users enjoy the benefits of this friendly little anchorage.

This carved tree sits on a main road going out of Paignton and was a 140 year old Monterey Cypress. It was 92 feet tall and well known in Paignton. Unfortunately the tree succumbed to disease and was cut down in 2001. Bystanders asked for keepsakes and the tree fellers rewarded them with slices of boughs. Paignton Zoo requested a large piece of the tree for the elephant enclosure. Seats and faces were carved into the surviving trunk and it remains a Paignton landmark.

Left: A wonderful sky seen over Broadsands beach whilst a lone child stands on the shoreline. Torquay and Thatcher Rock sit on the horizon.

The boating lake at Goodrington beach has pedal boats modelled on swans. On this sunny Summer's day morning a group of real swans were resting on the bank. Luckily I was early as when visitors arrived for the rides they left.

Opposite: A sunny late Summer's day at low tide, Goodrington beach.

Founded in 1882. The Paignton Club has a unique history in the South West of England. For more than 128 years it has been part of the social fabric of Torbay and its majestic Grade II architecture is a constant reminder of the great Victorian era. Situated at the southern end of Paignton promenade, and just a short walk from the harbour and town centre, the club offers members and their guests a welcoming and relaxing meeting place.

A greenkeeper chats to dog walkers whilst mowing the grass at the 'pitch and put' golf course above Broadsands. Wonderful views of the coastline can be enjoyed from here.

Bowling in the late Spring sunshine at Torquay Country Bowling Club. The club has been in existence in the grounds of Oldway Mansion since 1929, offering golf, tennis, squash and badminton in the 1920s when Oldway Mansion had ceased to be the Singer family's private residence. The bowls section started in 1930.

Opposite: Elberry Cove in Paignton is surrounded by lovely woodland walks. Next to the cove sits the ruin of the Bath House which is visible in the centre of the picture. It was built for Lord Churston in the 1700s, standing three storeys high. The ground floor flooded when the tide rose and his Lordship could swim through a gated doorway, preserving his dignity. The building also held a 'hot bath' where sea water was heated and pumped in to warm him up after a chilly dip.

From a distance, these pastel coloured seafront properties look like they would fit in at Babbacombe Model Village.

Previous pages: Oldway mansion and the gardens looking resplendent in late Summer.

This page: Around 1871 the Fernham Estate in Paignton was purchased by Isaac Merritt Singer, the founder of the Singer Sewing Machine Company. The old buildings on the site were demolished and he commissioned a local architect, George Soudon Bridgman to build a new mansion as his home. Isaac Merritt Singer died on 23 July 1875, shortly before work on the original mansion was completed. The mansion is modeled on the Palace of Versailles. The grand ballroom was the venue for social dances attended by, among others, Agatha Christie.

The Grand Staircase. Paris Eugene Singer, Isaac Singer's third son, supervised the alterations at Oldway Mansion between 1904 and 1907. The rebuilding work was modelled on the Palace of Versailles, and the eastern elevation of the building was inspired by the Place de la Concorde in Paris. The interior of the building is noted for its grand staircase made from marble and balusters of bronze. The ceiling of the staircase is decorated with an ornate painting based on an original design for the Palace of Versailles by the French painter and architect Joseph Lebrun. The ceiling is a replica painted by Carl Rossner, who studied the original by Lebrun before creating the reproduction.

It is not known when Kirkham House was built although the design suggests that it is of fourteenth or fifteenth century origin. This medieval house was bequeathed to the nation in 1960 by Ada Frances Jennings. It has been extensively renovated but many of its original oak beams and carvings can still be seen. It is open to the public.

Right: Goodrington Gardens sitting above the beach huts. Thatcher Rock can be seen peeking out beyond the headland.

A small boat sits in Paignton harbour at low tide on a warm Summer's afternoon.

The winding slides at Quay West Waterpark that towers above Goodrington beach.

Above and left: A very wide view of the Southern end of Paignton beach from the end of the pier. The harbour is around the corner to the left. The Paignton Club sits just left of centre and the new Apollo cinema is just right of centre. Inset is a closer snapshot of the part of the image with the Paignton Club to show the detail created by this technique.

Opposite: Paignton seafront looking from the pier. The attractive Villa Marina Hotel and the Redcliffe Hotel sit to the right. The Redcliffe building itself is unique. It was built as a private residence in 1856 by Colonel Robert Smith who served with the Royal Bengal Engineers and styled his home with a distinct Indian theme. 'Redcliffe Towers' was converted into the hotel in 1904.

View across Torbay from Roundham Head.

Opposite: This colourful seaweed caught my eye in the rock pools at the far end of Preston beach.

Early Summer flowers complementing the pastel painted houses on Paignton seafront.

Number 51 and Number 71, Paignton seafront.

A wonderful view across Torbay to Brixham on a sunny afternoon from the top of Goodrington Gardens. I particularly like the old iron railings in the foreground.

Opposite: I like, whenever possible, to frame shots. A gap in the crab and lobster pots allowed me to look through and compose this photograph of Paignton Pier.

This image shows the entire length of Paignton Pier taken on a very windy day. The 780ft pier, with its customary grand pavilion at the seaward end, was opened to the public for the first time in June 1879. It was financed by Arthur Hyde Dendy, a local Paignton barrister. The pier-head pavilion was home to many forms of entertainment including singing, dancing, recitals, music hall, and most famously Gilbert and Sullivan's comic opera, HMS *Pinafore*. On the death of Arthur Dendy Paignton Pier was purchased by the Devon Dock, Pier & Steamship Company, under whose ownership it became a regular stop for paddle steamers travelling between Torquay and Brixham.

In 1919 the pierhead and its associated buildings were destroyed in a fire. These were never replaced and a period of decline followed. Sectioned as a defence measure in 1940, for fear of German invasion, the damaged neck was eventually repaired once hostilities had ceased. In 1980 the fortunes of Paignton Pier took a turn for the better when a major redevelopment project was undertaken. This included the widening of the shoreward end to ensure a uniform neck, and the construction of the rather stylish pavilions that remain today.

People enjoy the sun and play with their dogs on Goodrington beach.

One of the colourful wooden shelters on Paignton seafront. Visitors take a welcome break from the midday sun.

Right: Shingle and pebbles on the steps at Paignton beach. The remains of a previous high tide.

Impressive architecture in Paignton.

Right: An atmospheric Winter sunrise at Paignton Pier.

Winter light casts a warm glow over Paignton Pier.

Opposite: A peaceful place to sit and read and enjoy the fantastic views across Torbay to Brixham.

The Paignton & Dartmouth Steam Railway runs for six and a half miles on the former Kingswear branch line between Paignton and Kingswear, Torbay. In 1972 the line was sold to the Dart Valley Railway Company. After leaving Paignton and passing Goodrington beach, it crosses two viaducts, one is pictured here, with a pleasant backdrop of the sea.

A very colourful and detailed panorama of Brixham Harbour from the quayside. Characterful cottages sit in the evening sun on the top of the hill overlooking the harbour.

BRIXHAM

On 5 November 1688, the Dutchman, William of Orange arrived in Brixham. His intention was to overthrow the Catholic King, James II of England. There were as many as 20 000 men and 5000 horses that landed that day. He succeeded in his quest and was to become King William III. His statue, erected in 1889, stands on Brixham harbour to commemorate the landing. The block of stone on which he first set foot is preserved in the base of the monument.

Left: Tranquillity at Brixham harbour showing the picturesque fishing cottages and fishing boats.

Berry Head is the site of an Iron Age hill fort that was mostly destroyed by the construction between 1794 and 1804 of the fortifications to defend the Torbay naval anchorage from French armies. The former artillery house now houses a public display. There were originally 40 guns but they were never fired in anger. Some of the original cannons can still be found here. This is an evening shot of one of the original batteries.

The *Golden Hind* in Brixham is a full sized replica of one of the most iconic ships from the age of exploration and has sat in the harbour since 1964. It has a long history of appearances in film and television. Sir Francis Drake, who is best remembered as an explorer, and in his most famous ship, the *Golden Hind*, became the first Englishman to circumnavigate the globe in 1577. The ship is open as a visitors attraction. The impressive glass tower of the new fish market is in the background.

Brixham Harbour with the newly completed fish market and its distinctive glass entrance to the right. The *Golden Hind* sits amongst the smaller vessels.

Traditional Brixham fishing cottages.

Opposite, top: A fishing trawler returns to port, passing the lighthouse on Brixham breakwater. Paignton seafront and pier sit in the background.

Opposite, bottom: A stone marker on Berry Head enables visitors to orientate themselves with distant landmarks. The lighthouse stands in the background.

BRIXHAM FISH MARKET

Brixham's fishing history stretches back to its early medieval roots as a small fishing port. It had grown by the 1800s to be one of the largest fishery centres in the UK.

The £8 million market replaces the old fish market which was built in 1971. The new market includes fish grading and display areas, a restaurant and fishmonger. The new fish market will help sustain Brixham's valuable fishing industry for many decades to come.

The Torbay Lifeboat sits ready for action on a calm day amongst the expensive yachts. Since 1866, Torbay Lifeboat Station, located in Brixham, has operated an all weather lifeboat. The crews have a proud history of life saving, with 52 awards for gallantry.

Opposite: Sunrise at the lighthouse on Brixham breakwater. The lighthouse station was established in 1878, and the current lighthouse has been there since 1916. It is approx 6m tall and made of cast iron.

Brixham harbour and breakwater from above the town, with the old lighthouse to the left and the new fishmarket to the right.

Wonderful late afternoon light on the neat rows of colourful cottages that overlook Brixham harbour.

Opposite: Tankers sit off Brixham at sunrise awaiting passage up-Channel.

Looking over Brixham harbour through the rows of lobster pots.

A fishing boat rests in Brixham harbour in the early morning light. Over one hundred fishing boats land and sell their catch at the local fish market. The fishing fleet is made up of large beam trawlers and smaller day boats. Some of the smaller day boats can actually be seen working from various vantage points around Torbay.

Right: Looking across Brixham harbour towards the newly completed fish market. Colourful Autumn foliage decorates the foreground.

Yachts sit and wait for open seas at Brixham Marina.

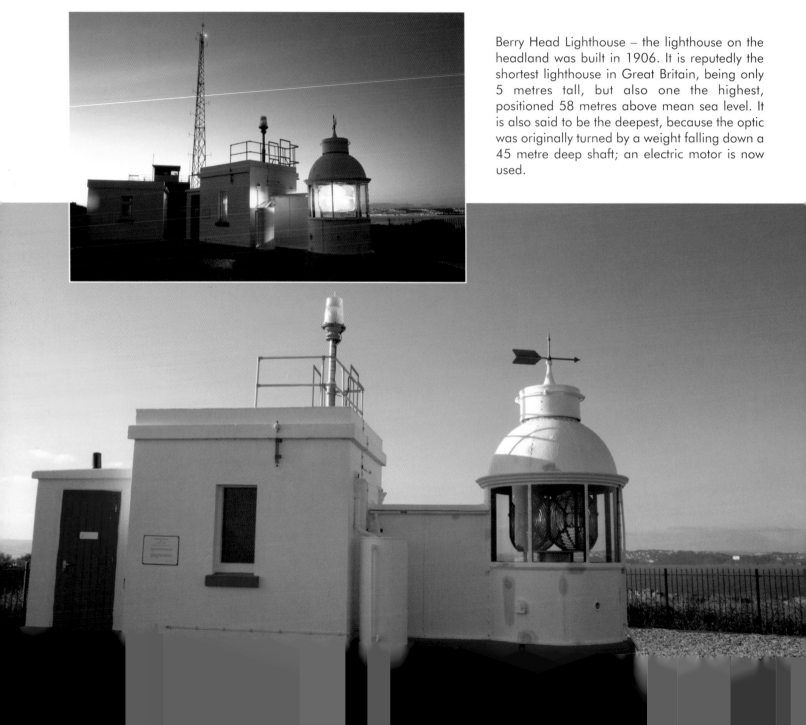

Berry Head Lighthouse – the lighthouse on the headland was built in 1906. It is reputedly the shortest lighthouse in Great Britain, being only 5 metres tall, but also one the highest, positioned 58 metres above mean sea level. It is also said to be the deepest, because the optic was originally turned by a weight falling down a 45 metre deep shaft; an electric motor is now used.

Brixham's Coffin House has a romantic folklore attached to it. Apparently it was built because a father did not like his son-in-law to be and he told his daughter that before they wed he would see them in a coffin – hence they built a coffin house and the father's wishes were met!

A photograph taken from above Brixham. Thatcher rock can be seen in the distance. It was such a clear day that Sidmouth, Seaton, the cliffs at West Bay and the Dorset coastline could be made out quite easily.

Opposite: Colourful terraced houses overlook Brixham Bay.

Overleaf: This photograph was taken in early winter from the cliffs at Berry Head. Filters were used to slow the shutter down to five minutes to capture the cloud movement.